CRASH INTO
THE DAY

CRASH INTO THE DAY

There is no time.
Lou Reed

Gary Zarr

authorHOUSE®

AuthorHouse™ LLC
1663 Liberty Drive
Bloomington, IN 47403
www.authorhouse.com
Phone: 1-800-839-8640

Front cover photo: Jefferson, NY, Gary Zarr, 2013
Back cover art: Gary Zarr
Cover design: Collin Arnold

Published by AuthorHouse   02/05/2014

ISBN: 978-1-4918-5779-3 (sc)

Flames and trains
and wings,
and planes and parks,
and fields and barns.
Schoolyards and clubs,
streets and bars,
diners and dreams.
And your special heart,
and mine too,
with so many others,
together
in the dance.
And now
I really understand:
No message
is
a message.

Signs

The hero has fought on against monsters, the mysterious ebb and flow of his energy and spirits, the grave doubts rearing to life over many years, across distant lands and through many adventures.

Now alone again, backed into a strange cave, the stars begin to appear, he sees his own breath in the air, realizes that a magic intervention of the universe itself, a lucky twist of fate, is needed.

Only this rare occurrence will save him, show him the best way forward on his singular, passionate, rich, yet lonely, path.

And although he realizes that these positive turns of events are the stuff of fables and fairy tales, foolish and childish to the hard and bitter world of men, his heart and mind will never give them up—for he remains unable to give up hope.

"Life presents gifts and marvels daily," he whispers. "We must remain vigilant."

He learned long ago that the mysterious, transformative powers of life are purposely hidden in the mundane details of each day.

Nothing can be overlooked. The stakes could not be higher.

So he reads each human face, examines every corner and byway of the road, embraces dear friends, touches each tree and animal, gazes into the eyes of lovers, scans the sea and sky.

Crouched against rough stone, his breathing becomes more even, his eyes slowly flutter closed.

Far away, in the night, there is howling.

Exhausted, he's not sure if he hears his own voice or another.

There will be a sign.
Every thing is a sign.
Every thing has meaning.
There will be a sign.
Every thing speaks to us, tells us what we need to know, exactly what we have been waiting for.

And at that moment, he began to dream . . .

Contract Killers

I see
the image
of a bird flying.

Reality is broken.

The answers aren't
in their usual places,
on TV, in books, in music,
in her face, online,
in the mirror, in clouds,
the sun, in conversation.
No one's calling
to fix it
anymore.

From the sound
of my heart
I know
it's time
to pull the trigger,
to hire contract killers,
patient, dedicated, resourceful,
possessing unerring vision,
prepared to hunt and kill
the real enemy,
inside,
strangling
my dreams,
my yearning
for ascension,
true freedom.

I see
the image
of a bird flying.

Eighth Commandment

What I say is real.
You are my destination.
Your heart beat
my train stop,
your beauty
where I must get off,
like silhouettes
of birds
when the sun
turns
soft orangey.
Touch me.
Here,
I touch you.
Step closer.
Accept
my world.
It is always
on fire
like the sea,
like these words.

Confession

You are
a haven
for me,
a sacred place
where gentle birds kneel,
pray on wet cobblestones,
a fresh morning hour
where singing starts,
a land of touch and sweat,
dreams and gentle laughter,
where I can
crash
into the day,
follow
the story.

Wherever

Wherever
I am
from now
till then,
always
there's you
near,
laughing,
holding on
tight,
unsure,
yet certain,
in the back
of the cab
on New Year's Eve
going home.

You Dance

Not laughing,
smiling
softly
at me.
You dance
as darkness
comes on.

Cloud Song

Endless carpet
of dark gray blue
clouds drift, puff,
wave, creamy,
insubstantial streams,
froth and laugh,
sing one last time
today for me
as the sun recedes,
lowers,
readies to rest
with a promise
to return
if we are good enough,
our hearts open enough,
have faith enough
for such brilliant light
tomorrow.

Brand Ambassadors

Being
a brand ambassador
the motionless Sphinx whispers
hoarsely for ages,
unheeded
by parades
of famous, forgotten civilizations
each with its expiration date.
With no specific
hieroglyphic
call to action,
his profound
meanings
were lost
long ago.

Venus-shaped
Coke bottles,
shiny, tattooed aluminum cans,
sweat and throb in our hands,
define our age.
Listen carefully.
You can hear
the universal chorus
of their high-pitched voices
explain who we are,
where we're headed,
hurtling too fast.

Elephant Parade

Scene 1
Profound,
faithful elephants
step patiently in lush unending jungle
on a bed of sleepy land mines
in gardens planted in a forgotten time of rage.
I can't bear
the concussive thuds
which I know will come,
which are always coming,
through the warm breeze
thick with dreams and blood.

Scene 2
holy shit 3am can't sleep
blood sprayed all over the living room
how'd it get there on the walls paintings coffee table the kitchen cabinets
I slip on a pool of darkening blood like a skateboard
Who's going to believe what I'm seeing right now?
can't breathe I race to the bedrooms to check
my daughter's face asleep my son's long legs asleep my wife's back asleep
they're fine thank god for now at least but
I can't imagine where this sea of blood has come from
Who is going to believe what I am seeing I can't even scream.

Scene 3
whoosh whoosh whoosh
whoosh whoosh whoosh
helicopters overhead
drooling my index finger
slowly draws stick figures with blood
on the scarlet TV screen

Now, that's a tree in blood and that's a man in blood.
And that's a girl in blood and that's the big red sun in blood
you know no one is going to believe this tonight
can't sleep my face smeared with this holy blood
sitting in a red pool on the Persian carpet alone
doodling pictures I learned in school somewhere
a herd of stampeding elephants roars through my brain
trumpeting too loud ringing in my ears aching
how can they rocket so fast crying with their blown-off stumps?
where is the enraged herd running with purple clouds swirling?

Scene 4

I'm trying to get it all down
oh my god oh my god
I'm trying to get it down
oh my god
we need the magic language now
I realize that no one can hear me
but we really need the magic language now
we really need the magic language now
whoosh whoosh whoosh
whoosh whoosh whoosh
incoming incoming incoming
we need the magic language now
we need the magic language now
we need the magic language now

The Cherry Trees

Unshaven, squinting through thick round glasses,
he shifted his heavy t-shirt pearshape,
so it was easier to stand
with aluminum crutches.
And so the story goes like this:
The two magnificent cherries
on each side of the path by my door,
about to explode
their pinks and reds and whites,
were planted
so he says, wheezing, smiling,
in his gray, baggy sweats,
by a Japanese diplomat
50 years ago,
in gratitude,
when different people
lived in our building,
when another war had just ended.
I know these two trees remember
capable hands
from Osaka, Tokyo, or was it Kyoto,
young roots placed into this shallow earth,
as generations have walked through the front door,
mothers guided shy girls into family snapshots,
their young beauty enflowered forever in spring
between the two growing trees,
and how over years
girls became mothers,
left our building and the cherry trees,
moved to the suburbs, to California,
far from how each
late April,
like today,
the world insists that we remember,

what we sense each day as we pass,
and pray for when we need good luck,
what the ancient poet wrote:
From this year on, you know the
Spring time, the cherry tree . . .
I wish you would never know the
scattering of your blossoms . . .

Merlin

It takes
blood
soaked
strength
to turn
anger
into
positive
things.

My Angel

Why
must
I wrestle
this angel
with a face
like my own,
in the dirt,
in the sky,
struggle
for so long,
confront
head-to-head
his relentless
stamina, power,
hard will,
an angel
who laughs
just inches
from my face,
ferociously
beats
his iridescent wings
to terrify me,
knowing
neither
of us
will ever
yield,
knowing
neither
of us
knows
why.

We Believe

How
we want
to believe
things
that are
not real
or partially so,
not
totally true.
We have to
hold onto
what we believe
to be
things
that seem
forever,
but aren't.
Like a kiss,
promises,
how eyes sparkle
when the light
agrees
with smiles,
conspires
with perfection
and beauty
to fool us
again.

Love

In
this
vast
world
endless
of ours
so little
room
ever left
to fall
out of
love.

T-shirt

For this
world
tour
Love!
is
the sponsor
of our
universal
pain.

Shepherd

I don't
need
soft
pillows.
Like a shepherd,
on my side,
I cradle
my own meadow,
a broken universe
covered in bones,
incandescent
dreams.

Dream Outcry

He fell back
like a statue
from the small round table,
shattered white,
when I told him.
Then it got me
from behind,
from above,
in a powerful full nelson.
Staggering
under its weight,
I struggled to breathe,
managed
to toss
a stone
through the dirty basement window.
Outside
the signs
cry
I need help,
which I'm shouting
as loud as I can
into a world
gone
sound proof.

The Train

I don't believe
that on this train
the stops
they designate
on the colorful map
above our heads
really tell us
where
we need
to stay on
or get off.

Fake Memories

In all this time
I realize
we've never had
a real conversation.
Just fake memories
are left
alone,
by themselves,
with what's in my purse,
with what remains in your wallet.
To the world
we're perfect
except that I always have
to see
somebody
about something.
I always need
to see
somebody
about something,
about so many
under promises,
so many
over charges.

A Reminder of Happiness

What you don't need
on this gray, official
start of spring,
still inside
with listless,
ambivalent snowflakes
falling confused,
as if winter still mattered,
as if the sun
would never return,
what do you don't need,
what you definitely don't need,
is a lover's touch
of loneliness,
cheerfully
conveyed
by phone
in the morning.
So you search the day,
explore every street,
tease out the tissues
of the ripe bodies of every moment,
with patience,
determination,
yearning,
hoping
for a reminder of happiness,
which appears,
this time at least,
rushing
on a bus
in a smile,
a look.

That Person Exists

That person exists
at least in your mind.
Here though he seems
to have gone away
like in a movie.
He just slipped
out of his own plot
into a chapter
he can't find.
I'm having oatmeal,
coffee, near the office.
All quiet, still,
because a new year's
arrived for some
though really new years
come each day
like fresh bread,
without celebration,
but we don't see them,
can't smell them,
are unable to fully surrender
to welcome them,
their joyous march
of chilly dawns,
the ceaseless cavalcade
of unannounced daily new years,
like lost, hungry children
without names,
waiting,
smiling at us,
expectant,
judging us,
by our capacity
to say
yes.

Reply to the Star of the New West

yes,
heart mountain,
trees make mistakes too
might get lonely
i suppose
but they're not really
mistakes,
they are directions,
approaches,
outreaches,
walks we take
with others who are special,
saunterings that end
in surprising,
yet understandable ways,
in separation,
which is inevitable,
and yet always surprises
(it just depends
how deep
the startling cuts
inside you)

one of my own walks,
extraordinary,
close, promising,
stopped today,
a very strong love
that can't be
any longer,
and so I suffer,
like you,
though we try
to teach ourselves
to harden
because all those songs
tell us

we have
to be
tough
enough
to love

so i do know what you mean
about this sense of being alone
whether among people
on or off the grid,
in paradise,
somewhere in between,
or just not sure
about where
or how
or why

yet I am convinced
we have to keep
our hearts open,
our minds clear,
our strength intact,
laughter and fire
firmly lodged in our belly

so that
again and again
we can
make what others
call mistakes
but what i choose to call
embraces of life itself,
vulnerable and honest,
strong and assured,
confused and yearning,
certain and ascending

otherwise,
we stop living,
searching for a heart,
and whatever we create,
ever do in this world,
has no spirit,
no soul,
will never take root,
barely cling to life
or thrive and flower
like the knowing trees

Red

Think
I gave
you
a copy
of that song
you said
you liked
so much.

The one
I think
we danced to
in Shanghai
while the little girl
got sawed
in half again
in the Midwest
magic show.

Think
I gave
you
that song
when we laughed
so much
in flaming red
silk robes
made love
at night
watched boats
in the harbor
and in the mini-bus
passed
dreamy black bulls
protected
in high grass
on steep mountainsides
in mist.

Summer Rain

Summer rain
love
as day ends gray
warm drops fall
splash far below
where I can't see
onto earth
New York
thirsty
for more
touching.

Rio

I still have
bits of things
from Rio
that belong
to you.
But they don't
know it yet,
poor things.
I will
bring them
to you.

Animals

There is
the unexplainable
grief
of animals,
majestic,
indomitable,
quiet,
humble,
solitary,
proud.
How this
complements
their constant
natural joy,
or our presumption
of their unfailing good humor
because we
are not
yet
worthy
to speak
directly
to them.

Dry Cleaning

When the Korean lady
checked her computer
to see if I was still there
after so many years
your name came up.
Head down, all business,
she smiled and spoke your name,
her glasses on the end of her nose.
Your name
suddenly alive in the world again.
"No, there's just me now,"
I said, quickly pushing my shirts,
a sport jacket, across the counter.
Frozen silent, I patiently folded my ticket
into a tight postage-stamp-size square,
hid it in the middle of my right palm,
rushed out
into early Saturday morning,
surprised at how
after all this time
the tears arrived
unannounced
under my shades
half-a-block away,
began to drown me
on the curb,
impatient for the light
to change.

Maybe Death

Maybe
it's about
don't be
afraid
of death.
The more
we knew
about it,
the less
we'd fear
it.
Maybe.
Maybe.

Parade

Instead
of you
it's me
this time,
standing
alone
on the float
in the parade,
the world
roaring
past.

Prayer as a boy
stumbles
into the death
of his great-grandmother

for Flossie

Here are three people.
Give them to her.
This way she'll have
the best time in heaven.

He always sat
next to her
when she visited.
The last time
he saw her though,
he knew.
And he hid.

Here are three pennies.
Throw them
into the water.
The fountain
will remember.

Not Fade Away

for Russ

When you start on your journey to Ithaka,
then pray the road is long,
full of adventure, full of knowledge . . .

Did you bring ice cream?
I don't want to walk now.
I don't want to walk . . .

We fade away,
if we don't
explode starlike before,
ripple and circle to nowhere,
outcries that tear the lacework of stars
to nothing.
End up,
we do,
silly in a wheelchair
with a black eye from a fall going to take a piss,
a colossus preparing,
as he puts it,
for a different adventure.

I don't remember names anymore.
My eyes are red, watery.
Did you recognize me?
Did you know me when you came?

Alone most of the day
with people we don't know,
unable to recall
the smiles, the sunlight on waves,
the great yellow windows thrown open on Samos,
piles of weathered books,
always Bach in the air and home cooked meals,
what rainy Paris at dawn felt like

These politicians are all crooks.
It's disgusting.
The world's all about money.
C'est degoutant
How much of this TV can you stand?

We can't visualize all the apartments, the favorite dogs,
the bars, stray cats we took in every summer,
all the songs, streets we walked,
wild conversations in cafes,
crazy times you don't even know the half of it,
the fight it takes,
the sheer will,
to be a free man,
an evolved man.

What do you think the food's like?
Institutional.
That means they fuck up everything.

Giacometti showed him his studio,
Siqueiros and Leger praised his work.
In Paris he threw a party for James Baldwin
to celebrate
Go Tell It on the Mountain.
Beauford Delaney made soup one time for him.
That positive review in Mexico—
"Best young talent in decades,"
drinking and making the scene at the Cedar Tavern,
the flowers in the piazza in Italy,
the kids laughing under the fountain in the garden,
driving all over Europe with two small brats
in the back seat and no money.
How those murderous jealous assholes
tried to put him in prison
under the Greek dictatorship.
But the ocean and sun
always sang what was important,
what you can't forget even if you wanted to,
whispered to him at night
when sleep never came,

what he must never forget,
what his mother softly sang
to him in his dreams
to protect him.

No lotion is left in that clear plastic bag.
They put it in the drawer.
It softens my skin.
Can you ask them for more?
Can you get me more?

It's when we know it's over.
As we fade from here,
as fatigue pulls us down,
yet energy suddenly bubbles
with just enough force
so we glimpse over the tray
with the antiseptic dinner we don't touch
that living is over now,
the real ballsy thing called living is finito,
and that even this fake bullshit living in the hospital,
this playacting living we do to make visitors happy,
will be over too.
Soon.

It's not funny.
It's not funny.
My right foot's swollen and it hurts like hell.
And I'm not going to rehab tomorrow morning
unless the doctor checks my fucking foot.
What's happening?
Forget the nurse—I want the doctor to check it
before I get gangrene.

Lovers,
at night in the room
he wants to touch you again,
and each stone of the walls and stairs he built
in the garden with the empty well and fruit trees.
Yes, all his lovers,
and the smell of the oil paint,

the brushes, the cans,
the lumber he used like a workman to make the frames,
the wet canvases pregnant with new worlds,
the crazy summer school on the island,
the dance, drama, poetry, painting, sculpture
laid out like a classical picnic
by the sea for the Love Generation to sample,
and how she came so young and tall and slender
to class one summer day on Samos,
and how she stayed for so long,
surprised him at times by her faith, steadfastness
and how he always wanted to protect her,
his muse,
his Penelope
until his last breath.

And who's that hunchback guy with the backpack?
I see him all the time going back and forth.
I see that hunchback all the time in the halls.

It's all happening so fast.
But in slow motion, too
like an old time comedy film—strange.
It's tough to keep up.
You never know
when it's really over.
It sneaks up,
even upon heroes,
those just getting by,
even clowns, even saints.
It's just—suddenly—*time.*

My foot's hurting like hell.
I can't sleep.
Can you press the button?
I want the bed raised.
Press it—there, there . . .
Did you bring ice cream?
You know I like vanilla.
I like chocolate, too.

And as the light dies,
we must remember
that the end of a life,
any life,
isn't all there is to the show,
isn't the fresh greeny spring
beginning of it
when everything in the world was innocent and new,
or the great thick, long middle,
glorious, chaotic, fiery,
twisting and turning,
full-force, extreme, painful,
brilliant, sexy, wily,
undeniable, rebellious,
that splendid magic torch
we each clutch in our hands
like deliriously happy children
shooting out into the world
a fireworks
display
meant to last
forever.

Young Love in Ephesus

The pulsing cicadas,
the beating of unseen waves,
was all they heard
through the wooden shutters.
Sweating on their flexible backs,
breathing hard,
satisfied in the hot world of their small bed,
that stolen night
in many-tongued, labyrinthine, endless Ephesus.
Secretly together,
they smiled in darkness,
jealously guarded what they alone held
while the marble colossus surged outside,
devoured precious goblets and rings from Egypt,
necklaces and spices from China.
They have everything imaginable,
his husky voice murmured
into her neck like the sound of an underground river,
except true love.
They have everything—except love.
She giggled, bit his lips gently with her pure teeth.
Their eyes glittered, full, hazy, floating, purring,
turning together,
turning over singly and then together,
turning over again and again,
until they were lost,
one at sunrise,
laughing and leaning
into the golden oasis
of their glowing young bodies.

Wacaville

We build for ourselves
and for the frightening gods we are able to find,
abandoned like plastic bottles and worn tires
in the empty lots of our minds.
Walls rise carefully,
simply, symmetrically,
to withstand The Lord of Tremors,
to enhance the extraordinary,
to connect us to special parts of nature,
to defiant rock outcrops,
cleansing, clear streams,
fragrant caverns shaped like jaguar and deer.
If we understand enough about
the Two Realities,
the true nature of pigs, roosters, bulls,
dogs, sheep, birds, the Milky Way,
one day we will be able to build
a rainbow bridge connecting
this world of tears and death
to the everlasting feast
kept so far from us.
And wherever we stand
will be an altar.
Wherever we laugh
a sacred grotto.

Bracelets

Her glamorous golden bracelets,
snakes coiled round sexy fashionable arms,
were not enough
to shield her
from the exploding mountain
that buried her
as she clutched armfuls of jewelry,
incinerated,
desperately holding beauty,
luxurious possessor,
memorialized forever
by a jealous and demanding earth.

Listen to My heart

We should make a date.
Otherwise it won't happen.
Life tends to slip
between our fingers
unless we clutch it
tight, squeeze it.
Don't let it get away.
Listen to my heart.
Don't let it get away
this time.

The Plan

So
share it
now.
Don't hide
for too long.
I need
to find
you.

Your plan
is healthy
and terrible
and it involves
me.
And I tell
myself
all good things
take time.
I say
all good things
take time.

And this plan
you have,
that you're
not sharing
involves me
although I act
unaware,
touch your knee,
smile into your eyes.

Because
I don't believe
that any moment
of my life
has ever lied
to me.

Your plan
is healthy
and terrible
and it involves
me.

Okx

It's not the best for us.
I agree *Okx* too fast.

This Saturday morning
I recall her lips saying
You are my heart,
and I'm certain Charles Aznavour and Stevie Wonder
see into our souls,
even when they're asleep
and just their faint breath sings to the night,
reverberates with Nina Simone, George Jones,
Jacques Brel, Amalia Rodrigues
into every dusty corner,
sweeps through every littered alley,
recognizes young and old,
poor, rich, in villages, slums,
high rises, London, Mumbai, Miami, Toronto,
Paris, Hanoi, Cuzco, LA, Beijing, New York,
sees deep into us all,
into our off-the-grid escapelands,
our pop mental waste sprawls,
these hip-hop flip-flop
reel-a-state-of-minds.

It's not the best for us.
I agreed *Okx*,
too fast,
inevitably,
like a wisp of smoke,
dancing,
vanishing
in the wind,
in places we met,
that lovers
always
seem
to find.

Bird in Flight

She brought
music
into my lost world,
and sorrows too
from long ago.
I patiently
tracked down
each raging ghost,
refused to let them
come between us.
And as our world
slowly grew,
flowered finally
like spring,
it suddenly died,
an unlucky bird
that never had a chance,
shot down
over New Jersey,
the marshlands,
where animals teem,
where we try
to build over.

Heart

The heart,
a little box
we shutter,
protect,
when life pokes
carelessly inside,
roughly,
too deep,
for too long,
to pain.

Heart,
a golden box
we will open
one day,
recognize
the moment,
a smile,
the arms,
the hair,
the neck,
the back,
the legs,
that moment.

At least
that's what
I try
to imagine,
today.

Degrees

The degree
to which
you
can get
outside
your
head
is
the degree
to which
you
are
finally
free.

Birthday

The more
I live,
the less
I know.
It's about
the essential
feeling,
about
ascending.
When I close
my eyes,
breathe,
try to find
it,
I'm always
in the sun
beside the sea,
looking out
past the waves,
to that line
where sky
and sea
kiss,
embrace,
become one.

Thanksgiving

Walking
in warm winter rain
to catch a cab
in early morning
darkness
I see
it takes
enormous strength
to feel
true
gratitude.

Notes

Contract Killers
The title is a riff on an album title by hip hop artist, the Ikonik.

Note Fade Away
The opening quote is the beginning of the poem, *Ithaka*, by Constantine Cavafy, translated by W.H. Auden.

The Cherry Trees
The final lines are by the Japanese master Ki no Tsurayaki (872-945).

Wacaville
My late friend, Dr. Craig Morris, explained that the Inca covered their vast empire with *wacas*, powerful yet delicate architectural creations intended to mark and extol outstanding aspects of nature; they created a spiritual network of constructions meant to acknowledge and elevate the arresting faces of the universe made manifest here on earth for us to acknowledge.

About the Author

Gary Zarr comes from New York City.